You Are There!

London
1666

Dona Herweck Rice

Consultants

Timothy Rasinski, Ph.D.
Kent State University

Lori Oczkus, M.A.
Literacy Consultant

Publishing Credits

Rachelle Cracchiolo, M.S.Ed., *Publisher*

Conni Medina, M.A.Ed., *Managing Editor*

Dona Herweck Rice, *Series Developer*

Emily R. Smith, M.A.Ed., *Content Director*

Stephanie Bernard/Susan Daddis, M.A.Ed., *Editors*

Robin Erickson, *Senior Graphic Designer*

The TIME logo is a registered trademark of TIME Inc.
Used under license.

Image Credits: Cover and p.1 Yale Center for British Art, Paul Mellon
Collection, USA/Bridgeman Images; p.4 Falkenstein Heinz-Dieter/Alamy Stock
Photo; pp.6–7 Illustration by Luc Fontenoy/Pudding Lane Productions, Game
Art BA, Leicester Media School, De Montfort University; p.10 Imagno/Getty
Images; p.12 Hulton Archive/Getty Images; pp.14–15 Illustration by Timothy J.
Bradley; pp.16–17 Wikimedia Commons/Public Domain; p.21 National Portrait
Gallery, London, UK/Bridgeman Images; p.22 Tristan Fewings/Getty Images for
Royal Institute of British Architects (RIBA); pp.24–25 Science Source; p.26 Martin
Beddall/Alamy Stock Photo; all other images from iStock and/or Shutterstock.

Library of Congress Cataloging-in-Publication Data

Names: Rice, Dona, author.
Title: You are there! London 1666 / Dona Herweck Rice.
Description: Huntington Beach, CA : Teacher Created Materials, [2017] |
  Includes index. | Audience: Grades 7-8.
Identifiers: LCCN 2016034998 (print) | LCCN 2016035398 (ebook) | ISBN
  9781493836161 (pbk.) | ISBN 9781480757202 (eBook)
Subjects: LCSH: Great Fire, London, England, 1666. | London
  (England)--History--17th century.
Classification: LCC DA681 .R53 2017 (print) | LCC DA681 (ebook) | DDC
  942.1/2066--dc23
LC record available at https://lccn.loc.gov/2016034998

Teacher Created Materials

5301 Oceanus Drive
Huntington Beach, CA 92649-1030
http://www.tcmpub.com

ISBN 978-1-4938-3616-1

© 2017 Teacher Created Materials, Inc.

Printed in China

WaiMan

Table of Contents

Warm London Night, 1666

A hot, dry breeze **wafts** the yeasty scent of baking bread down Pudding Lane. Most residents of the city sleep inside the tightly packed homes that line London's narrow, cobbled streets. But in the stifling **byways** on this September night, cats howl, rats scurry, and countless homeless citizens huddle in doorways and alleys. Though their lots in life are challenging, today they are grateful simply to be alive. Twenty percent of London's population has died over the past two years. A deadly and painful **plague** has ravaged the city throughout 1665 and even unto this date—September 2, 1666—a day that history will long remember.

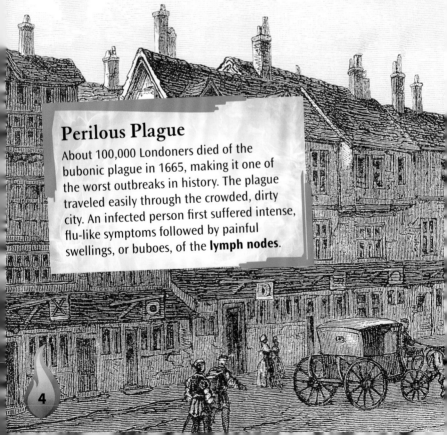

Perilous Plague

About 100,000 Londoners died of the bubonic plague in 1665, making it one of the worst outbreaks in history. The plague traveled easily through the crowded, dirty city. An infected person first suffered intense, flu-like symptoms followed by painful swellings, or buboes, of the **lymph nodes**.

While the city sleeps, Thomas Farriner's bakery shows signs of life. The staff has mixed, rolled, and baked their wares, preparing for the morning's customers. Customers they will never see. Because on this hot night, no one notices a wayward spark from the oven…until it is too late. And the city burns.

The Facts

The Great Fire of London began at Thomas Farriner's bakery on Pudding Lane, just past midnight on Sunday, September 2. Farriner, a baker for King Charles II, lived upstairs.

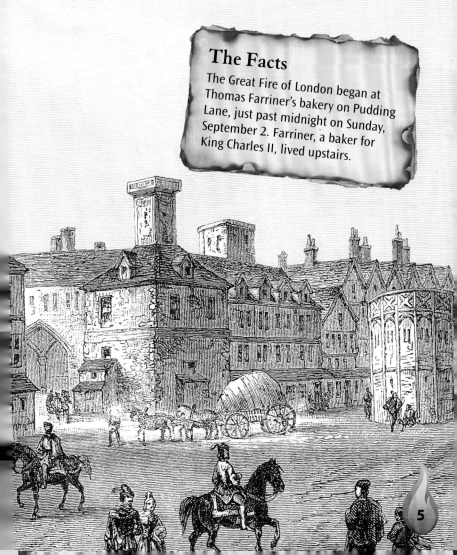

Inside the Bakery

The summer of 1666 had been unseasonably dry and windy. The land was **parched**, and the people felt parched, too. Disease had ravaged them, and they were tired, worn out, and fearful of what may come. The reign of Death—an **indiscriminate** reaper—can do that to people.

Saturday, September 1, dawned as dry and windy as the many days before it had been. The people felt stifled in the suffocating city streets, where their tightly packed houses fit together like pieces of a patchwork quilt.

Thomas Farriner's bakery was similar in many ways to the warehouses that surrounded it. The wooden buildings were crowded and highly flammable. The timbers themselves were dry as bone from months of parched, dusty weather.

With the right conditions, everything could go up in smoke. As a single chime from the clock tower heralded the hour early Sunday morning, the right conditions had fallen into place.

An Eyewitness Account

"It made me weep to see it," seventeenth century diary writer Samuel Pepys famously wrote of the Great Fire of London. His home was a few blocks from Pudding Lane.

A Common Concern

Most homes had open fires every day for warmth, cooking, and light. It makes sense, then, that accidental fires were common. Candles would tip over, sparks would shoot from the hearth, and clothing could easily be dragged through a flame. Fire was a daily hazard.

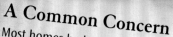

THINK LINK

- House fires were common in the seventeenth century. Why do you think that was?

- What are today's common fire hazards?

- What precautions against fire should people have taken at that time?

Wake Up!

After raking coals from the ovens and—they thought—**extinguishing** the embers, the baker and his staff retired for the night. Unaware of the troubles sparking below, Farriner and his family slept soundly upstairs. But downstairs, a manservant was startled awake. The air was thick and clouded, and what was that he smelled? Smoke! It filled the bakery. The servant lunged from his bed, calling out to a sleeping chambermaid, warning her to awake. Disoriented and fearful, he rushed upstairs to rescue the family. Whether exhausted from the day's work or affected by the **engulfing** smoke, the family members were difficult to rally as precious moments ticked away. By the time they were up, the spark had **ignited**, hungry flames devoured the bakery, and all possible escape routes seemed severed.

But what about the maid? Perhaps she was blinded by smoke, blocked by fire, or immobilized by fear. She never left the bakery and died in the consuming flames. History does not remember her name—the first **casualty** of the great fire.

The family was more fortunate. Someone suggested using an upstairs window, and they escaped directly into a neighbor's bedchamber. From there, they crawled along the neighbor's roof to safety. Although Hannah, Farriner's eldest daughter, was badly burned, all members of the family and their manservant survived.

Sizzling!

A piece of pottery that melted in the fire on Pudding Lane is on display at the Museum of London. Tests on the pottery show that the fire's heat reached an intense 3,092°F (1,700°C).

Who Did It?

Robert Hubert, a Frenchman, confessed to being a spy and starting the fire. He was hanged for the crime. He said he threw a fireball through a bakery window. But it turns out he couldn't have done it. The bakery had no windows, and Hubert wasn't even in London at the time!

9

In their panic while escaping th...
the baker and his family probably ...
heavy gale whipping past them. La...
gusting wind roared across the Eng...
headed toward London. Thatched ...
corn, while chimneys were knocked ...
the bakery burned, the gale roared ...
shooting hungry sparks in all direc...

Across from the bakery stood th...
Street. Hay bales on the property w...
for the fire, and they quickly burst i...
crept and leapt to Thames Street, w...
teeming with flammable goods lined...
coal, alcohol, and highly **combustib**...
warehouses, fueling flames with eve...
to stay alive. Many buildings burned...
Others caught fire and, in single bur...

The Problem with Pitch

Pitch, or tar, was commonly used
as insulation for poorer Londoners'
homes in the seventeenth century.
Unfortunately, it is highly flammable
and added to the ease with which
London burned.

The blaze continued toward London Bridge and west across the city. London, at the time, had no fire brigade or any organized system for fighting fires. So, panicked citizens scrambled to put out the fire, using leather buckets of water and water "squirts." It was like **dousing** a forest fire with toy water guns. Their tools were no match for the intensity, **magnitude**, and frenzy of the flames.

St. Magnus Falls

The church St. Magnus Martyr stood at the head of London Bridge, where it had been since the Norman Conquest of 1066. Churches were common throughout London, and St. Magnus became the first of many to burn.

Failed Leadership

The fire moved shockingly fast and became too powerful for the people to extinguish. They soon abandoned their efforts and ran in desperation to save their families and belongings.

As the fire spread, local **constables** decided that the Lord Mayor should be notified. They wanted to pull down buildings outside the burning area to create a firebreak to stop the flames. They would do this using fire hooks, or long metal poles with hooks on the ends used to demolish buildings. But only the Lord Mayor, a merchant named Sir Thomas Bludworth, could make this decision. The constables woke Bludworth, but he was angry and did not agree with them. He said there was no need for drastic measures—and he returned to bed.

At sunrise, just hours after the **inferno** started, about 300 homes were already burning. Light from the fire could be seen 30 miles (48 kilometers) away, and the gale from the east raged on.

Sunday Trouble

The fire started on a Sunday—a day of rest for most people. Workers along the Thames who otherwise might have been around to quickly put out the fire were instead in their homes at the time. This early lack of involvement helped the fire spread.

It wasn't until the evening of Sunday, September 2 that the demolition of buildings was finally approved, but by then, it was too late. The fire was overwhelmingly powerful, and it easily jumped the rubble-filled firebreaks. It was now a firestorm, and it was completely out of control.

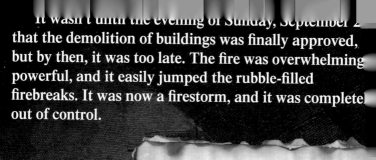

Sink, Bury, or Burn

People fled outside the city or to the Thames, but they couldn't carry all of their belongings. To try to save their valuables, some people threw them in the river, while others buried them. The diarist Samuel Pepys wrote that he buried his wine and cheese.

Fear Fuels the Flames

Monday, September 3, dawned to a raging inferno burning northward into the heart of London. People panicked, and fear spread as quickly as the flames. Rumors began that "untrustworthy" foreigners had started the fire. England was at war with Holland, and the Dutch were the country's enemies. Many Londoners turned violent against the Dutch because they believed that a Dutchman had deliberately started the fire in his own bakery. Others believed that the Catholics from France had attacked the city, despite there being no evidence of an attack. The French were similarly sought and beaten. In fact, mobs **rampaged** throughout the city and turned violent against anyone they thought was foreign. Instead of fighting the fire, they fueled their own hatred and fear—and in doing so, helped the city burn.

Looting broke out everywhere, in shops and homes alike. People trying to flee the fire were blocked by outsiders coming into the city, trying to sell their "assistance" to the frightened masses at highly **inflated** prices. In the first two days of the fire, London was infested with some of the worst aspects of human nature.

Pepys, Pigeons, and Parties

In his diary, Samuel Pepys describes a haunting image of pigeons flying above the flames, singeing their wings, and plummeting to their deaths. At the same time, Pepys was hosting a party. While the city burned and the pigeons dropped, Pepys's guests were "as merry as at this time we could be."

Saved in the South

London Bridge crossed the Thames and was tightly packed with buildings. Half the bridge burned quickly, but a gap in the buildings on the bridge stopped the fire from crossing south of the Thames. What caused the gap? A fire had already burned that section in 1633.

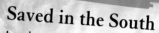

"The Very Pavements Glowing"

Londoners thought things could not grow worse, but on Tuesday, September 4, they did. The fire made its way to Guildhall, the seat of government, and set the place ablaze. But it was the taking of St. Paul's Cathedral, the city's religious center, that proved a heart-wrenching blow for all. Confident that the grand old church with all its stone and lead would withstand any fire, local printers and stationers had stuffed the building with books and papers in an attempt to save them. Instead, they served as fuel, and St. Paul's went up in a shattering roar. Londoners were horrified to see a **molten** stream of lead running down Ludgate Hill, on which St. Paul's Cathedral had sat. One man later wrote that he saw "the very pavements glowing with fiery redness."

But then, miraculously, thankfully...**reprieve**. The military was ordered to use gunpowder to demolish houses around the Tower of London, which kept the fire from spreading eastward. And on Wednesday, September 5, the gale that had been blowing steadily began to die. Losing its greatest ally, the fire grew weak. On Thursday, September 6, it was finally controlled. Although it would **smolder** for many weeks, the Great Fire of London finally came to an end.

Melting and Crashing

The heat of the fire was so intense that the lead in St. Paul's Cathedral liquefied within just 30 minutes. The molten mass ran down the stonework walls, breaking them apart. As the walls crumbled, they crashed through the church floor and into the **crypt** below.

Blood Moon, Sea of Fire

Londoners reported that the moon glowed a deep blood red throughout the days of fire. And people 40 miles (64 kilometers) away said the fire roared like waves crashing on a shore. They also saw a strange, frightening glow hovering over the distant city.

ruins of St. Paul's Cathedral

Damage Done

As the flames died, Londoners came out of hiding to survey the wreckage. A large portion of London was destroyed and up to 80 percent was damaged. Although records say only six people died in the inferno, this doesn't seem likely. It's possible that deaths among the poor and middle classes were not recorded. It's also possible that the fire so thoroughly consumed the bodies that nothing remained to be identified.

In all, about 13,200 homes were destroyed, leaving at least 100,000 people homeless. Around 87 of London's 109 churches burned to the ground. About 400 streets were wiped out.

Thousands of people were financially ruined and lost everything. Many went to **debtors' prisons**, which were soon overflowing. The cost of the damage done to the city was about 10 million pounds. To put that amount into perspective, think about this: the average person's income at that time was about 5 pounds a year.

A New Danger

During the winter months following the fire, bands of thieves took up residence in the burned sections of the city. They looted anything they could find and dragged people from the streets into empty cellars to rob and beat them.

area affected by fire

area unaffected by fire

area where fire started

N

RIVER THAMES

STOP!
THINK...

Use the map to answer the questions.

◎ How do you know that an easterly wind fanned the flames of the fire?

◎ What role do you think the Thames River had in stopping the fire?

◎ What considerations should city planners have made while rebuilding the city?

Rebuilding Begins

During and just after the fire, Londoners set up temporary shelters, such as tents and shacks. But some were not so temporary and were used for years. Many such shelters offered little protection for London's citizens, resulting in deaths during the coming winter. King Charles II encouraged the homeless to move away in an effort to avoid a rebellion.

Much of London had to be rebuilt. The king appointed six **architects** to redesign the city. Christopher Wren (later "Sir Christopher" because of this work) was placed in charge of churches. This included the redesign of St. Paul's Cathedral in its same location. The new cathedral was completed in 1710 and still stands today.

The fire's emotional and psychological effects on the people of London are hard to measure. Samuel Pepys wrote that he had nightmares for many months and ongoing stomach problems. His wife's hair fell out due to stress. He also tells of a church visit shortly after the fire during which the entire congregation wept.

The political and social climate remained hostile for a long time. Many people continued to believe that Catholics had started the fire under direction of the pope, the church leader. The tension would last for many years.

Not Again!

Another fire in 1676 burned more than 600 homes on the south side of the Thames.

Sir Christopher Wren

Major Losses

The destruction of several important public buildings dramatically impacted London's economy and communication systems. These include the Custom House (import and export of goods), the Royal Exchange (center of commerce), and the General Letter Office (post office).

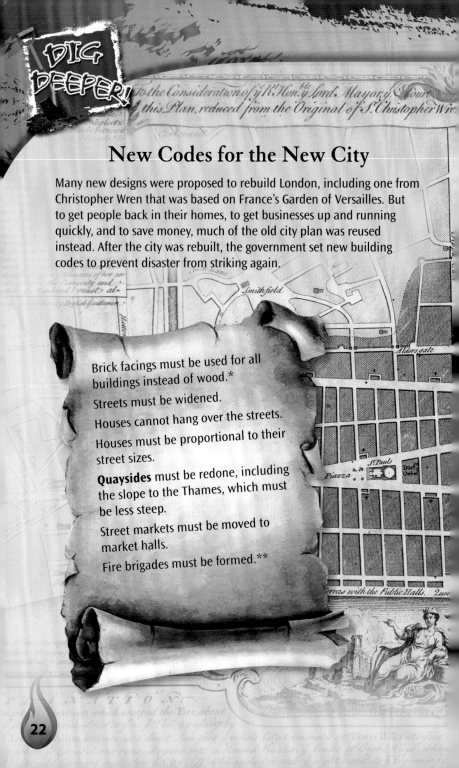

New Codes for the New City

Many new designs were proposed to rebuild London, including one from Christopher Wren that was based on France's Garden of Versailles. But to get people back in their homes, to get businesses up and running quickly, and to save money, much of the old city plan was reused instead. After the city was rebuilt, the government set new building codes to prevent disaster from striking again.

Brick facings must be used for all buildings instead of wood.*

Streets must be widened.

Houses cannot hang over the streets.

Houses must be proportional to their street sizes.

Quaysides must be redone, including the slope to the Thames, which must be less steep.

Street markets must be moved to market halls.

Fire brigades must be formed.**

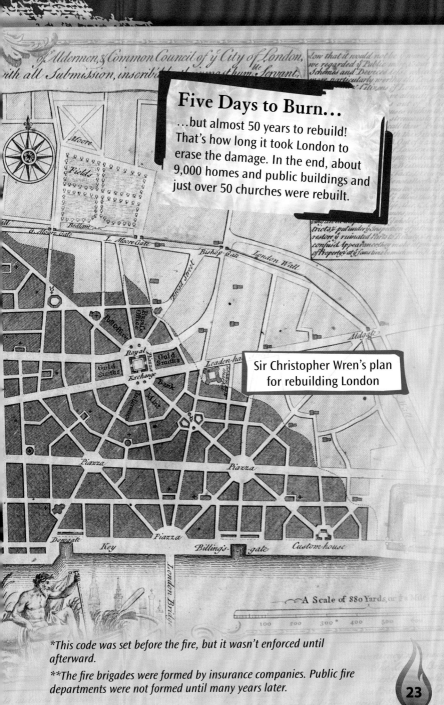

Five Days to Burn...

...but almost 50 years to rebuild! That's how long it took London to erase the damage. In the end, about 9,000 homes and public buildings and just over 50 churches were rebuilt.

Sir Christopher Wren's plan for rebuilding London

A Scale of 880 Yards, or ¼ Mile

*This code was set before the fire, but it wasn't enforced until afterward.

**The fire brigades were formed by insurance companies. Public fire departments were not formed until many years later.

Oh, Rats!

Rebuilding was not the only change to London in 1666. The deadly plague that had ravaged its citizens vanished, quickly and quietly.

Why?

For many years, people believed the Great Fire of London ended the plague. We now know that fleas on rats carried the disease-causing bacteria. Rats were everywhere in the crowded, filthy city, and their fleas had easy access to Londoners. Many of those rats and fleas **perished** in the fire. Since the plague diminished so radically at the same time the rats died, the connection from the fire to the end of the plague is a reasonable one to make.

But scientists today aren't so sure this long-believed explanation is true. The plague diminished everywhere, but the fire only occurred in London. How could that be if rats and fleas were the carriers?

Though we may never know for sure, it's possible that people had begun to build **immunity** to the disease. Since each new outbreak of plague was smaller than the last, the immunity theory is a possibility.

Goodbye, Plague

The Great Plague of 1665–1666 was the last major outbreak of bubonic plague in Great Britain.

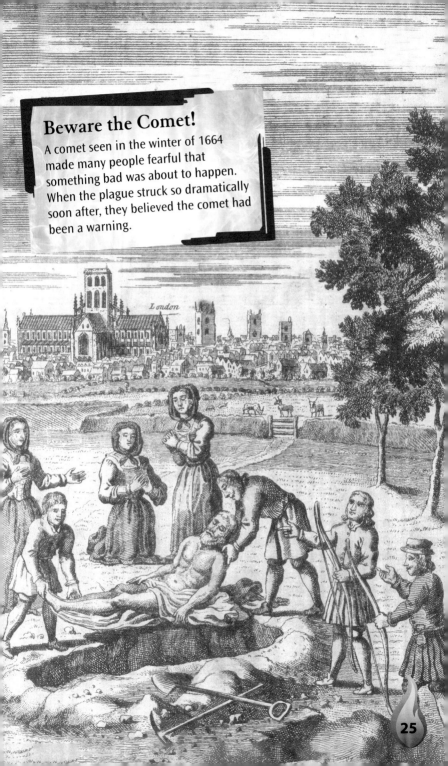

Beware the Comet!

A comet seen in the winter of 1664 made many people fearful that something bad was about to happen. When the plague struck so dramatically soon after, they believed the comet had been a warning.

London

Where Are They Now?

Thomas Farriner rebuilt his home and bakery and continued his work until his death on December 20, 1670. He always contended his innocence, and he was never found guilty. But in 1986, members of the Worshipful Company of Bakers in London met on Pudding Lane to offer a plaque to the city. The plaque acknowledges that their fellow baker, Thomas Farriner, was, in fact, the guilty party.

The spot near where the fire began was marked a few years later with a 202-foot (62-meter) column called the Monument. Visitors can climb a narrow staircase inside the column to a lookout at the top. Engraved on the Monument are sculptures that show what happened during the fire and what caused it. The Monument declares that "the hand of God, a great wind, and a very dry season" are to blame.

And what about London itself? In the years after the fire, there was a renewal in Londoners' attitudes about the city. One man wrote that London had become "not only the finest but the healthiest city in the world." In the many years since the Great Fire, London has seen its share of troubles, but always, the grand old city has renewed itself while holding on to its traditions. Like the phoenix, it rises from the ashes and sits confidently on its battered but steady perch.

Oh, and let's not forget the rats. They came back. They always do.

In Memory

The Monument is the tallest freestanding stone column. Not only is it 202 feet (62 meters) high, it is 202 feet away from the site where the fire started. Each year, more than 100,000 people climb the 311 steps to the top to enjoy magnificent views of London.

Who's to Blame?

An original inscription on the Monument blamed the fire on the "treachery and malice of the popish faction," meaning Catholics. Though this suspicion lasted, the inscription was removed around 1830.

Glossary

architects—people who design buildings, both for style and for stability

byways—side streets that are not used often

casualty—person who dies

combustible—flammable; able to catch fire and burn quickly

constables—police officers

crypt—enclosed tomb

debtors' prisons—jails to imprison people who cannot pay what they owe

dousing—pouring or spraying water on a fire

engulfing—flowing over and covering

extinguishing—putting out

ignited—caught on fire

immunity—the ability to keep from being affected or infected

indiscriminate—affecting or harming many people or things in a careless way

inferno—a very hot fire

inflated—made too large or high

looting—stealing things during a war or other destruction such as a fire or riot

lymph nodes—glands in the body through which nutrients, fluids, and waste material are carried between bodily tissues and blood

magnitude—size and extent

molten—liquefied by heat

parched—very dry, especially due to hot weather and lack of rain

perished—died

plague—a deadly disease that spreads quickly to a large number of people

quaysides—river banks

rampaged—moved wildly and in a destructive way

reprieve—a period of relief

smolder—to burn slowly, without flames but usually with smoke

wafts—moves gently through the air

Index

Check It Out!

Books

Charles River editors. 2014. *The Great Fire of London.* CreateSpace Independent Publishing Platform.

Clout, Hugh, ed. 1999. *The Times History of London.* Times Books.

Ellis, Peter Berresford. 1986. *The Great Fire of London: An Illustrated Account.* New English Library.

Hooper, Mary. 2004. *Petals in the Ashes.* Bloomsbury.

Porter, Stephen. 1996. *The Great Fire of London.* Sutton Publishing.

Turnbull, Ann. 2013. *Forged in the Fire.* Walker & Company.

Video

Tom Bradby. *The Great Fire.* Ecosse Films Limited and ITV Global Entertainment.

Websites

The National Archives. *Great Fire of London: How London Changed.* http://www.nationalarchives.gov.uk/ education.

The Great Fire of London. http://www.greatfireoflondon.net.

Try It!

As a historian, one of your tasks is to research and then compare and contrast similar events over time. In this reader, you learned about the Great Fire of London in 1666. More than 200 years later, in 1871, there was a fire in Chicago, Illinois.

- Research the Great Chicago Fire. How did it start? How long did it last? What residential or commercial areas were damaged?

- How many people were affected? In what ways? What rescue efforts were made? By whom?

- What characteristics of the two fires are similar? What characteristics are different?

- Make notes and citations from your findings.

- Present your findings in a format of your choice using visuals (graphs, charts, or diagrams).

About the Author

Dona Herweck Rice has written hundreds of books, stories, and essays for kids on all kinds of topics, from pirates to heroes to why some people have bad breath! Writing is her passion, but she also loves reading, live theater, dancing anytime and anywhere, and singing at the top of her lungs (although she'd be the first to tell you that this is not really a pleasure for anyone else). Dona was a teacher and is an acting coach. She lives in Southern California with her husband, two sons, and a cute but very silly little dog.